T0290184

BEWILDERNESS

ESSENTIAL POETS SERIES 265

Canada

Guernica Editions Inc. acknowledges the support
of the Canada Council for the Arts and the Ontario Arts Council.
The Ontario Arts Council is an agency of the Government of Ontario.
We acknowledge the financial support of the Government of Canada.

BEWILDERNESS

CATHERINE BLACK

GUERNICA EDITIONS

TORONTO • BUFFALO • LANCASTER (U.K.)
2019

Michael Mirolla, general editor
Elana Wolff, editor
Cover and interior design: Rafael Chimicatti
Cover image: Marlee Jennings, *Floating Suburbia*
Guernica Editions Inc.
1569 Heritage Way, Oakville, (ON), Canada L6M 2Z7
2250 Military Road, Tonawanda, N.Y. 14150-6000 U.S.A.
www.guernicaeditions.com

Distributors:
University of Toronto Press Distribution,
5201 Dufferin Street, Toronto (ON), Canada M3H 5T8
Gazelle Book Services, White Cross Mills
High Town, Lancaster LA1 4XS U.K.

First edition.
Printed in Canada.

Legal Deposit – Third Quarter
Library of Congress Catalog Card Number: 2019930424
Library and Archives Canada Cataloguing in Publication
Title: Bewilderness / Catherine Black.
Names: Black, Catherine, 1975- author.
Series: Essential poets ; 265.
Description: First edition.
| Series statement: Essential poets series ; 265 | Poems.
Identifiers: Canadiana 20190049081 | ISBN 9781771833998 (softcover)
Classification: LCC PS8603.L246 B49 2019 | DDC C811/.6—dc23

For the boys

Contents

In a forest of question marks
you were no bigger than an asterisk.

— CHARLES SIMIC, *The World Doesn't End*

This Is About the Forest

The trees screech like violins. The air is a kind of coloured sugar. The white birch screams or sings in falsetto above the others. When the river is listening she's a good listener, but otherwise she's self-absorbed and goes on and on about herself. Once in a while you'll see a cardinal and his mate in the brown-grey forest of spring. Squirrels scuttling branches will give you a crawly, queasy feeling you'll want to brush off by rolling in the new grass. But the soil is damp, so you don't do that. You'd get all graceless. If you peel some of that bark off the shrill birch, you can make yourself a little mask of it, a paper mask, and you'll haunt the forest with your tattered eyeholes and luminous face. That would be something. Scare the rabbits onto their rumps, watch them stretch out in terror, then feel apologetic. That will kill an hour or two. But let's not talk about you. This was about the forest.

Marooned

The month of June was sullen and mute, a depressed relative at the dinner table, forcing smiles. The lake was such an anxious grey that even the boaters wanted nothing to do with it and spent their hours in contemplation of their miniature television sets, wishing they lived in Malibu or on Gilligan's Island. Once, in the afternoon, there was a sunny break and the maître d' on the Moby Dick floating restaurant played hula music over the PA system. But only for a moment. Then the sun was smudged out by clouds and the maître d' was embarrassed by the rubbery ukulele and turned the volume down. Then off. There were only the sounds of water, televisions, a laundry line, a sail rigging vaguely clattering as it was pulled. The lake wished it were Caribbean blue. The seagulls wished they were poetry professors. The sailors wished they were debutantes and woodsmen. The clouds wished they were mountains. The sun wished it were a concerto. The green buoys wished they were islands, and the red, sirens. The Canadian flag wished it were a parachute, and the jib sail, a teepee. The pier wished it were Corsica. The bigger fish wished they were propeller blades, while the little fish wished they were bubbles. The waves wished they were wild horses. The little boy wished he were a fisherman and the fisherman wished he were a bullfighter. So it was in sullen June while everyone waited for July.

Hummingbird Incarnation

If I live rightly there is the possibility that I will one day transport the nectar of the hibiscus in my needle throat through Mexico.

In Mexico, they are smaller but faster and with more vibrations per minute than their sluggish Canadian counterparts.

If I live rightly there is the possibility of red dye instead of blood and the narrow proboscis and the enveloping pink of the hibiscus. There is the possibility of being so small in Mexico.

In Mexico, they hover audible. A swat sound. Faster. Feathers the emerald phosphorus of beetle carapace. Heart the tiny palpitation of a pea-sized red sack.

If I live rightly there is the possibility of the feathering of my body, its bones, made brittle. Its blood, made nectar-sweet.

In Mexico, there is the possibility of afterlife amnesia, forsaking this bulk and these moods. For a single singing rush of sugar.

Through the Telescope

Dream of San Miguel and a balloon man to wobble into view, like a colourful sea creature. Lumpy, riotous bits dangling and drifting from him. Then the spinning woman on stilts, twirling with lace sleeves drifting, no one watching as she orbits you, rapturous. Then your mother calls in the middle of everything. The scene in the square suddenly depopulates and the shadows retreat and the woman in stilts lifts off the head of her costume and underneath she is plain and maybe a bit sad, a bit sweaty, and the balloon vendor sits down and takes the bunches of balloons from his back and lights a cigarette, and the cowboys remove their hats and fall asleep on the benches, and the business people come out not to eat *helados* and not to walk arm in arm, but to rush from here to there, café to bank. These things happen not incrementally, but all at once. All at once the taxis disburse and the birds plunge into sculptural trees. There is nothing left on the breeze. It is scoured clean. The music is thin and the church bells stop ringing. Two lovers engaged in a kiss withdraw their tongues from each other's smooth mouths, and, suddenly aware of what they were doing, wipe their mouths with the backs of their hands. This is what happens when your mother calls in the middle of a dream of San Miguel.

Punting

Out there is a great silence of water. A crossing made from rooftop to rooftop upon floating suitcases, the buckles, barnacled. Instead of a new levy, the citizens have built rope bridges and boats of mattresses. They punt and put everything submerged onto stilts: houses, supermarkets, schools, casinos. The children learn their times tables five feet above sea level. Beneath them, the starfish count themselves: onefish, twofish. When the school bell rings, the children descend ladders of rope to find their parents bobbing wearily on overturned chairs, or sometimes, impressively, on sofas.

Mansions of Plywood

They are building a city of parchment across the park. They are building mansions of plywood. The men, like fever visions, clamber all over the roofs. I watch carefully and see that they wear cardboard hardhats, and one man swings a hammer made of smoke. They are raising scaffolds of mist to stand upon. They are building car parks of sand that will melt away with water. They are waiting for rainfall to paste together the seams of their paper neighbourhood. They have assembled walls of newsprint and flour, plugged garden beds with twisted tissue-paper blooms. They have shingled the roofs with cotton for winter. They have baked chimneys of mud and ash. I have watched them looking over blueprints of vellum and chalk, hands tracing imaginary lines, the foreman's words evaporating on his tongue. In the end, only the small oceans inside their blisters are real.

Meeting the Garbage Man

Meeting the garbage man's clamour, she asks to throw in everything herself. *Shouldn't let you*, he says, but something about her pulled-tight housecoat convinces him. Her slippers are getting wet. Petals from the crab-apple tree pasted to them. *Please*, she says, no question mark. Then everything overturns into the metal hoe of the garbage truck: Marxist manifestos, panama shirts, bad ski sweaters, sincere letters of apology and complaint, the splay-bristle toothbrush, silky sleeping bag, the map of Algonquin Park, the red towel, the shabby robe, the Underwood typewriter, pressed flowers from the pages of the dictionary, toenail clippings, hibiscus tea bags, pillowcases, a string of Christmas lights, the leather trench coat, the vintage car calendar, the woolen socks, the photographs of then, the emptiness of now. She doesn't wait long till it all turns over into the mass of other couples' soiled plastic bags and tomatoes and diapers and receipts. She doesn't wait long till it's all turned under in the mash of other days and waste.

Some Other Country

—for M.J.B.

She leaves her house of seashells and cotton wool, dolls and pillows, house of found wood, barn board once swollen with flash-rains of August. She leaves her house of batik pattern, house of well-thumbed books, house of heat wave, no fans, loose tea and manikin house. Of all she's collected, best are those things abraded by daily scoldings on the shore. I don't know Canada in this way. No islands in my periphery. These are the driftwood and shells of her some-other-country. Neither do I know the honest nets and bluffs, the grain waves and sputtering tractors, fractures of rock rising out of humming foothills. These are other people's poems. I know only the logic of my city's grid, Queen Anne's lace and chain link fences, firecrackers thrown between apartments on a suddenly meaningless evening. I want to write about the still inlets her home inspires, jetties and dolphins alongside her dinghy. But these are someone else's poems. And this is someone else's home.

A Home from Nothing

I assemble nests of glass and ash, nests of cigarette butts and pigeon down. I know the panic of assembling a home from nothing. Feather my nest with cigarette cotton. Down from a thistle. Fence grasses and synthetic yarns. Copper and brass wire. Strips of Goodyear rubber. A nest made by the Lakeshore, where the tide brings our tattered bits back to us, re-gifted. Nest of driftwood and condoms. Nest of mud and feathers and duty-free wrappers. Nest of thread and axel grease. Nest of false eyelashes, weaves. Of spider-web, spray glue, glitter, and spit. Nest of beeswax and screws. This is my edge-nest assembly. I wrap round and round these trappings picked from ditches of Birmingham Street from the lips of Lake Ontario. Edge-nest, where we softly roost, where we make do, make home.

Northern Mother

—for J.B.

Where's mother? North in her northern home, east on winds of goose down and starlight. Mother with hammock of wicker and fires blooming, throwing wild sparks from the mouths of chimneys. There in her cloud of moth's dust. There in the steam of melting sugar or sweep of chocolate dripped from paintbrush. Bones of fire, twirling double helix. She's strung white berries from doorframes. Juniper pricks her hands as she arranges boughs, twists cedar, winds wired ribbon with her unchanging, changing hands. Where's mother? There in white plumage of a pale bird on snow, in its peck, its red retina. There in blue shadow spilled across snow, calligraphy from a wire fence, there in fur of winter's animals, wrapped warm in a coat of white, guard hairs lovely and translucent, deep downy underneath. Where's mother? In houses of gingerbread, behind panes of candy, dusting confectioner's sugar from her pant legs. Now on Glebeholme, watching rain from her perch on the front porch or waiting for men to fix the crack in the city street, chewing tar from their twirling drum. There, holding sugar cubes for the milkman's horse, she's letting snow land on her tongue, she's opening a box with a red ball-gown inside, something her mother cannot afford. She is breathing in the smoke of a thousand cigarettes, exhaled from sofa, from father, from mother. She has driven downtown. She's looking for a bridge. She is buying bags of silver lipstick tubes and black lacquered compacts and jars and pots of pigment. She's dyed her hair another colour. The ever-changing colour of brass keys and inner fires. The ever-changing mother colour of then and now.

October Chronicle

September may have had its moods, but October is obsessing: throwing black handfuls of ink onto lakes, shattering the mirror, powdering and tarting-up in silver glitter, then gold, washing it off, glimmering now pale, glistering now pulling on a thick black veil. Feeling ugly, a prima donna waving cirrostratus away like gauzy thoughts of white-suited lovers from hot climates: so quickly dull, always disappearing sooner than you'd like with still so much to assume from their appearances. October is finally asleep in a chair, her horizon heavy with some dour prognostication, something left over from a tantrum, while far above, everything hums clear and cool as ether, sweet as a sleeping pill dream.

Liminal

—for E.M.

All those zeros, crossed in the middle so you won't mistake them for something else, something more than doughnut hole, more than coffee rim, loop of Hickman line. And your chronicling of every sealed delivery from the kitchen, the obscenely serrated carrots, steamed broccoli, the tin-foil covered apple juice, plastic-sheathed forks. For now, you know everyone by eyebrows and glasses, mouths covered by accordion paper, elastics over ears. The nurse calls me *sweetheart* and most certainly calls you that too. Tells me to scrub and how to scrub and that the door is pressurized against everything outside of it: microbes and germs and breath, spores and smog. You chronicle sunsets and sunrises and your unchanging view of Hamilton Harbour with all its good intentions and failed dreams and new growth. The sunset makes it look like Venice sometimes, and at sunrise you could be anywhere. I think of Jean-Dominique Bauby in his bone-trap with living eyes, how he skimmed forests and dove deep into the memory of lovers' mouths. I wonder where the cicada song and cardinals' vain repetitions took him. You, you are sealed from sound. The harbour could well be singing an aria, all the steam pipes and factory exhausts a carousel organ, chirruping, hooting. I could tell you anything, that the lake is full of sirens today or that the houseflies have begun to whistle. Your room breathes in and out with the sterility of a nurse. Your dreams must be full of aromas: cinnamon cardamom cut grass coffee linseed oil patchouli boys skin dust lignin. Your dreams must be full of things other than all those pierced zeros.

Polka Dots

What would we find in the straw grass, the baking grass, but dolls' heads with eyes bleached pink and lustrous? We would find their sunburnt irises. Hair all matted, a thing a girl-child combed out with morning fork, left egg yolk there on a good day, nothing to speak of, otherwise. On the porch, a mother elevates her ankles and sells *cold water*. Down the block some men are puzzling an engine and gunning jokes, ignoring tourists with camera phones and ironic tattoos and German accents. Charred beams and a lucid dream about dotting the neighbourhood with paint. He started raking trash and they called the cops on that kind of lunacy—what would he unearth, why disturb the universe with a comb? She, in her kimono, sits sidewise in butterfly-eye sunglasses while I wipe my nose and hold my distance. I retreat and work too hard to remember what is happening so I forget everything. Earlier there was refraction. We shattered some, and inside our shadows we cooled prism light from broken mirror. The paint and the nails and the outdoor congregation of stones in chairs, the word Dabl on the brain, dabble, dribble, daub, dip, drip, dripped—dripped as if it weren't so hot and dusty, a throat attack of *oohs* and *ahhs*. We do not find these places. They rise up before us, a sacred hallucination.

Dream of the End of the World

In the dream, a tsunami that tumbles us like a fistful of dice. I end up in a junk heap, atop lost glasses and bins full of Super 8 film, all unspooled. A woman tries to sell me a tchotchke from the trash. A butter dish in the shape of a hen, overpriced for the end of the world, I tell her. I try to make a long-distance call, but everyone knows you can't use a phone in a dream unless you're trying to call the dead. So, I am told by the operator to try again in a half hour. The lights in the city are all out. There are no cars in the mall parking lots, and a few people are circling, full of grief, on their bent bicycles. I kiss the telephone man when I return. He tells me his name is Charles. A small kiss. I know I'm married. Someone suggests lover's lane with my husband, which is much darker now, minus the light pollution.

It's Over

I've ended my relationship with the summer and the stars are sulking. Whatever. When I pulled the blinds to the night creatures they let out a winnowing whine, an unwinding sound. Their trill goes on all night sometimes—you need to block it out with goose down or toilet paper twirled into tips.

Night candles burn out, those stillborn entities, sucking oxygen from our sleeping mouths.

In summer, we were lean and tan, breathing deeply, churning on trails and through water. Now in a move to conserve heat, we walk slower, roll over in bed and sleep another five minutes. We dig ourselves deep under bedclothes. We huddle.

Morning will bump against the window, belly first. Leaves will tremble against blue and the jays will blast each other with slights and provocations. Slanted light will fall on the hedge, a slapdash paintjob. Thinning, the forest will grow underpasses and hidey-holes and every bare crevice will be plugged with stringy grass and clumps of dried leaves. The squirrels, in panic, will provoke anxiety in every other creature, while people in their homes will stockpile good wood, dry and sweet-smelling.

The children will bundle. We will grow fatter as summer leaves us. We will turn away from everything outside ourselves. It's over. We end it just like that.

Broken Butterflies

Trick a butterfly into telling you the location of the sleeping trees in Mexico, where they layer like lies and fall to the windshield rain-pummelled but with still-breathing wings. Do you know they have brains and heartbeats? Do you know their spindly legs terrify them too? They walk on them like brand new stilts. She told me.

The burrs of her eyelash legs on finger, sweet nothings. I try three times to free her on Queen Anne's lace, then bring her home. Try strawberry juice in dew drops inside her terrarium. When we open the curtains to the day she pumps, one full, decorated wing, one withered. Butterfly blood in tiny veins and ventricles. Butterfly heart. Butterfly muscle. One antenna crooked as a pulled stitch.

That morning my son and I were hand-in-hand looking for unshaded places, her life infusing sunshine. Finally, she hit the wind like a riddle. Sprinting, bent, goofy with joy and injury.

I write this with sun on shoulder blades, a different set of wings. Writing, a different kind of pumping blood.

In Backyard Sheds

Hibernate with the spiders in the sleeping sheds. The smell of dry wood and crickets, the web smell and oil smell of resting tools. Father's hands held the handles, wore the handle of the leather-wrapped hatchet, smooth as a chestnut. Fling spiders from your succulent arms, pale girl. Hold their contemptuous looks in the web of your irises until some man comes along and with a pinch and a flick clears out that look. A sound of sweeping is what will keep you awake all night. How much it sounds like sleep, like breathing.

The Deer and the Dictionary

All of nature stepping circles around itself on spindly fawn legs. Tamp down the ground with hooves and too many adjectives.

Trespass

I.

In the stem-root of the barn—that part left over from fire or years of quiet erosion, rain, or snow pressure, the prying of thumbs, or bumping rumps—we step the labyrinth of partial walls and duck thick wooden doorframes. Entering as into a mausoleum, a museum, a mineshaft, we point out little things, the date in a fallen cornerstone, the butt-end of a broken bottle, hand-blown and drained, the trough where horses dipped their muzzles to drink. We imagine the chug of their thirsty throats, we imagine outbreath. The pigs were happy here, the cows cocked a hoof in repose, and lazy-swatted fat, black flies. The mortar and fieldstone still recall construction-hands and trowels with thumbprints and whorls. The sun enters to illuminate the down of weeds growing here, like a field entered politely at first, tentative seeds through a broken-down door but now inside, it sprawls, slouches like an unwelcome houseguest, a drifter, a derelict. In the farmhouse, lacewings and dragonflies dart. Tag tails alight with shimmering wings, leaving behind on little elbows of broken grass the sputum-like froth of their trillion eggs. Stringy garden snakes are still and taste the air for our skin-scent. Down beneath the overgrowth, grasshoppers spring from our steps as we walk to the ticking of their hard bodies against the stalks.

There is the smell of our sunburns, the sunlight on grain, the smell of the sweat on the backs of our necks, warm denim, cigarettes, shampoo and muddied shoes. We are new weather moving through.

II.

Touching inside a ruined home is like touching inside a house of wax, or the parlour of some nervous aunt, or in someone else's wedding photograph. It is touching in a hothouse before a naked orchid. A hand on my belt buckle, and he is taller with heavier breath and more lung. He smells of bristle and salt, of flushed skin. He smells of copper and smoke, of blood and breathes this—caustic and delicious into me. The farmhouse, full and alive, takes a stamping, a shuffle of shoes before we lie like unknown others who were stripped of petticoat, suspenders, layers of skirt and a hand here, there, a stocking. We imagine how insects and lovers alike have draped their silken threads here. And when it is over, we are scratched red. There were thorny things at root level and small bugs that took our blood to feed their young. Our shoes, nosed together, look drunk and our pants with the heavy belts are in leaping poses against the trampled stalks. Naked in the farmhouse on a yellow afternoon, a hawk alights and suddenly we are made shy by his black beak and our pink skin. We startle him to flight and reassemble, tie shoes. Then outside the broken walls and webs, we see how the field has quietly birthed a silo.

Uncanny

We picked rhinestones from wings of sunglasses and searched the golden tongues of shoes for white lies or pennies that might have been left behind. I was outside when the manikins began to breathe. Down in the basement a wedding gown wept, not for her innocence, but for her dissatisfaction with knowing. A hat with false cherries laughed uproariously, a whole row of slips perspired around the underarms, while underneath the tattered carpet, a postcard thought of a good comeback two decades too late.

At Auction

He pinches at the circular nests of the spider's young, beneath the chair we'll buy at auction, the auctioneers in their cowboy hats and nobody-coats, their everybody-coats, and we all listen as he repeats *Wedgwood, folks, all real Wedgwood.* Mother sashays across rooms like a debutante, it doesn't matter that the floor is sewn with peanut shells and sawdust, barn wood or travertine the same to her sensible heels. The suitcases of the dead are packed with tiny records and antique jars, empty of home-made jam, travel diaries and postcards sent from friends who lived abroad, the smell of pomade, the military hair-brush. I wonder if it's possible to hear the sound of the war inside some of them. I'd hold my ear to their bristles if the locals weren't watching so politely from the corners of their eyes. Later, I tilt the salt cellar, flip the tiny spoon of grains onto a brocade of birds that erupt, squawking, now red, now blue, in flight over the armoires.

Moon-Minded

Let's be honest. The moon is sick of taking all the blame for this, blood tides pulled to our surface as she scrapes round the solar system looking for an out. It's all I can do some days, to fight her maddening hurdy-gurdy call to lunacy. We talk to each other more on these full days, our syntax, a mishmash in translation. Shadow girls, the two of us. Me, *one who slept too long in the moonlight*, always flicking such withering looks her way. I used to call her mottled mushroom, wrinkled my nose at her. Now visible in ruthless daylight, she's everywhere smirking, watching arteries surge, levels rise. My words to her grow crisp and crumble, leaf-like. Forever subtext in the way she speaks at me. I always want to leave our conversations before they're through, the way I leave meditation as I tumble into the abyss of beingness, jerk back from it like catching my chair from falling. I leave parties in the same way, in a quick and fretful, too-soon way that leaves me forever unfulfilled, a little lonely, if I'm being honest. Some days I could hide behind her visibility, two sisters, one more remote than the other. But which one's which? Stoicism's always been a family trait.

Water Piece

The morning she surfaced was calm. Everything—the road, the lake, the car mirrors and sunglass lenses—were *verre églomisé*. The light in patina, the rippled sky, silver and peeling. The lake murmured, rubbed its hands together, paced a little to shore, turned back only slightly, then again to shore. Only the lake knew for twelve hours, but didn't know what to do about it. Who to tell. It was ashamed to be implicated, to be made the mute accomplice. The lake was sleeping when it happened. Trusting its dreams. Turning over at its dark premonitions. And by morning, exhausted, it had begun to pace. To shore and out. To shore and back out. Bikes rolled by on the pier. The city was quiet. There was the metal clap of newspaper boxes. The lake ran with cold currents, mulling over. Running deep, and cold, and mulling over.

Meandering

I went out wandering with my dog and radio and all I could find was a frost-cracked compass and a prospector's hand, rigid with ice. Crisscross tracks in the snow, obliterations of perfection. The interception of the bounding marks of the fat grey squirrel, a rabbit. All this a kind of handwriting over top the narrative arc.

Semi-Industrial Morning

Morning, and again the noises from underneath, the creaking of rebar as it is pushed to bend, and the frog song burbling of sumps where the run-off from brass bullets pools. A ruffling of feathers as something takes flight with great jointed wings and deeply muscled arms.

Deep in August

All lawnmower blade and mirrored lens, you are tinted sunset reflected in chrome, you are sex song of crickets and the nest where my lover laid me down. You made me blush with your flat paddywhacks of sun when I slept on my belly, you drifted me on inflatable promises and lovelore over lakes at the speed of overhead clouds, like neither of us was moving. We drove north to you. Swam to the bottom of the lake where the rocks were glazed with ice and the fish had frosted eyes, and surfacing, you singed our lips when we came in close for a kiss. Surfacing, you shamed us so.

Bloody Moon

Nail to the tooth, chewing moon, remembering you, big and bloodied, over the harbour of my dirty city: coal stacks, power lines, and tall strangers. What you gave me was belief that things could be lovely just across the water, and I don't care if it was pollution or the drink, you were beautiful.

Forcing Poems

I've been forcing poems again, which is like gripping the crocus bulb and screaming at it for a spring flower. I dig at the meat of acorns and root around in the winter earth for tubers of poem, and come up with the dead finger-bones of a long wizened shrub, something I killed last summer with too much water or with negligence in the heat wave. Stir your ice-cubes and look on. *My, what pretty gardens.* I force poems from the moon like begging it for a sonata when all it sings are sea shanties and maybe the occasional hymn, but deeply off-key, tone deaf. I force poems from the panties of girls passing by, which is to say, I force poems in a perverted way, in a way that should have me incarcerated, and the girls, they provide nothing. They don't even flip their skirts to moon me. There have been other attempts that are just as damning, just as ridiculous. I demanded a poem from the subdivision one night as the snow came down in blots that hypnotized drivers on two-lane roads. I asked the identical rooftops for something monumental, something universal, and what they gave me was a kind of sideways glance and then they kept on in their suburban dialect, a conversation I could only make out from their swallowed burps and harrumphs. They closed their curtains in a manner most egregious. I got nothing, and deserved it. I demanded poems from the power lines where the children ride their bikes and the starlings are energized, lines that sizzle and pop like words. I got this funny sunburn on my cheeks from gazing up, imagining tightropes strung between our circus lives. Nevertheless, I will persist with my requests of the stony shore, the lighthouse, the bawdy yachts, the garrulous sea become tempest, become Lake Ontario. She's bound to give up something—if only the dead man's chest of zebra-mussel shells, and maps to other places.

There's Another Slant of Light

Early autumn strange. Light through wool of moody clouds, more silver and slant, like mirrors hung in the woods, like the glint of twenty thousand soup spoons. Houses look prettier in this light, people too, wearing bed-crease morning faces and crumbs of breakfast toast on their sweaters. I do love people sometimes. How can you not.

Contrapposto, Royal Ontario Museum

I leave my students in a carapace of crystal, in an enamelled box, under the alabaster scarab wing. They blink in their perfect languages of signs and symbols. I lose them near the Rosetta Stone reproduction, by the painted sarcophagus and they emerge in suits of armour. They emerge in snake scales and stand in contrapposto, drinking from goblets of hammered gold. I leave my students in the slotted archives, in the felt-lined drawers, in the cracks of the amphora. They emerge in the palm of the archivist, small as clay beads, small as butterfly pins. They have all been numbered. I lose my students in the cafeteria line-up, in the oversized elevator, in the mouth of the flying frog, by a lake that no longer exists. They emerge in shoes of lava, from the belly of the mud woman, from a long sleep inside the anaconda, from the diorama of the forest, where animals stare in perpetual alarm.

Scream in the Rain

Rain in the rain and the rain on the rain and the rain with the big dumb trees breathing out poetry like dope smoke, *wooo* they say, and last year the slice of a gypsy's earring in the amethyst sky, hanging over trees like an ornament too high, and this year the rain on the rain and the folded slickers of poets thinking white noise and the sizzle of microphones, trees strain to hear, the rainwater on my lips, no thunder, of course, no reason to leave, just shushing and squelching and mud on my motorcycle boots, others with umbrellas and children, while we have stoned trees and stage lights, poets with thick glasses studded with raindrops, and stories of fever and mindlessness. If you squint your eyes, the stage will blur into a bull's eye. I'm sure glad you're not the boy with the umbrella, and I'm not the girl with the microphone. I'm the girl with the wet lips in the oil slick, and the motorcycle boots and the mud and the memories of being stoned and stumbling and skinning knees, straining to hear what's under the white noise of rain and rain and shush and pinecones and microphones and poems.

Snowbaby

Jack Frost baby in the snow. How delicately tinged with blue, how wafer-pale against the ermine of another mother's shawl. Winter comes in drifts and with wolves that beat against the snow as they leap and snap. Disturb you with their claws and paws and recklessness. Disturb your careful bed. This rock-a-bye so harrowing.

Vows

The wedding in the green hills. The supermoon calling a howl from all of us, a howl we suppressed as we cleared our throats twice. Three more minutes till we're early, we said. Heavy chains in the distance held the lake back from the pier—you could hear it grunt against the strain. Someone opened a picnic basket, and doves, ravenous for love, erupted in an orgy. Such commotion in the needling pines, such gossip ensued. Shielded faces of chicks and children, a bent wing, a perfumed hand. Wind rippled the lake blue-grey and backwards. Think of: moment before rain or stroking the underside of an arm. We examined ourselves in tiny mirrors in our purses, spoons, mirrors of each other's eyes. We pulled pin feathers from our hair where they had started to grow or were left over from a pillow. We waited for vows. We waited for the tumbling of the moon. We waited three minutes, till we were early.

Conversations in the Attic

So gather in the attic where the heat off steamed milk has risen, and lower your voice, lean in, talk over your moustache, talk over top of your pale lips. There's a tilt to the attic, the house sags in the middle. Marbles from a child's hand will rocket to the centre of the room. Lower your voice as we talk of big firms or childhood, mergers or marbles. One of the problems of the attic is the view. It's perfect. And this can really worry you, particularly as the tilt of the room starts fucking up your equilibrium. You're gonna start to walk with a tilt, imperceptible at first, but then you'll start to notice the sole on one shoe wearing out, your clothing hanging to one side, a longer sleeve on your left arm, those sorts of things. But come on up to the attic and we'll talk. Hush yourself a little. Mouse-breathe and whisker-talk to me. One of the problems will be your desire to scream, but that feeling will pass eventually. Mice don't scream. I suspect they have dainty lace doily conversations about edible things. We'll do the same while you lean in to me.

King Bee's Crown

I've broken the king bee's crown, and his orb has rolled from the hive, lost in the underbrush where flocks of sparrows conspire with cheerful faces to commit treason.

Mimico Snow

Snow flying in the sun, whirling from some great vent under the earth. Light has flat edges, crystalline and sharp. Snow will not land on the ground today, so people outside will only walk through it, not upon it. Everything lifting and clean, only the mud is stuck in place, but just barely. It too might pick up and release itself. The shingles might peel back and flap away with grey pigeons. Mimico, place of pigeons, where thin chimneys huff wispy smoke that disappears two feet from the factory roofs. The sun burns through the atmosphere and insists it's spring, prematurely. Inside the perfect rows of matching houses are imperfect families and tilting Christmas trees and housecats with dirty habits, and untrained dogs that leap upon visitors at the door. Inside my imperfect home are plants and moths and too many views that leap and snap at visitors.

The Ritual Is Dangerous

The tremors quicken and the bees swarm in their sticky footed mass. My skin is a thing of paper nest, my head a hive. Not with thought but with resistance to weather. They have always said that bees sting and allergies swell with the coming of a thunderstorm, with the swim of humidity so sweet on clover wind. Tonight, the ritual is a slipping of thorns through slippers, under the nails of my toes, an itching of camel fur on the inside of my bedtime clothes. Tonight, the ritual is dangerous. I'm seeing ghosts and have been too long enraptured with the glowing bodies of TV stars and Hollywood socialites. When I close my eyes, I see them phosphorescent on my mind's screen. Tonight, the ritual is empty. I am stripped of all my inner meat and wear over myself the bristles of thistled things. What is that? The inner itch on the underside of bones, the squeaking of finger joints extracting words, and worst of all, the nakedness in front of the writing window.

The Wasp

Two wicked rice paper wings unfurl, the insect curls in
slick contraction, clings with sticky legs, a pulse of poison,
and in a quick-swatted sting the saffron-pinched thing
punctures a whole world with its hot pin.

Outgrowth

The outflowering of the chrysanthemum causes them incredible cramping. But you wouldn't know it unless you looked at them closely—those tightly-layered petals and that long-suffering look.

A Country Life

Why don't we go for a ride in the car? We could drive to the country and look at houses that might freeze us all winter long with those peculiar old-house drafts that seem to have no source, no busted windowpane or split door, but seem to run in a current, cold, down the thin staircase that leads to a kitchen at the bottom of the stairs. I will be the loving wife, elbows on the table, fried eggs and aprons, picking up your discarded gestures. And you can be my dog. I will be glad when you rest your chin on me, enough of a reward. We'll stare at the windows with curtains stained with the smoke of three thousand cigarettes, smoked in dejection by someone's loving wife who wondered over and over but never said aloud, *Is this it? Is this all?* You'll hate the cadence of my voice by the fourth or fifth month, depending on the extent of our conversations. Some men have hated my whistling first, calling it tuneless, some have fallen out of love first with my singing voice, and that's an understatement because there have been men who have hated my song. The sound of rain. We will be without it for months, even as the snow melts and the weather turns warm enough to drop water instead of ice, there will be no sound of rain as we sit in the felt of our living room. We'll be afraid that it will never sound of rain again, not with the incessant chatter of my thinking, nor with the fast movements of my multitasking hands, the thump of your tail. Why don't we go for a ride in the car and I'll show you a future never made for us? Just north. Not far from where we are right now.

Bad Weather

The dripping city, sock-thin, silk-grey. Its graffiti, a plume of embroidery. Day hangs damp and deflated. Skyscrapers are wet. Their good posture makes them look foolish to be out without umbrellas, all of them staring into the distance and never at each other. Droplets of rain slither students with puddle shoes and dripping backpacks, parkas. The cars move along their own reflections, insecure on rails of white light, leaving trails of red. A blue umbrella bobs across the street. Distance hazes and attempts to explain that far off somewhere there are fields being soaked and coming alive with fragrant dirt that might as well stand up and shake themselves off. Birds are gone. They melt with water. Children are inside their cardboard firetrucks and plywood kitchens with no running water. In the background, they listen to the weatherman endlessly tisk and scold.

Out Back

Somebody's been sitting where the thistles purple and point, where the striped cat claims land with piss, and somebody's been thirsty out there. She's been in the hammock drinking vodka from plastic bottles, the kind that rumple into refuse before you've even taken the last swig, right there in your hands. Somebody's made a home of rubbish and weeds. Somebody's crouched and shat. Somebody's listened to the neighbourhood dogs call to each other. Somebody knows the language of our shrunken wilderness and this she won't translate.

Lakeside Park: Some Instructions

Start feeling the ink and paper in its first contact, old lovers, and listen to the sounds around you. Start there. Start with the fat housefly looping by in search of sugar or shit, then follow the hollow-rush of jet plane overhead in pristine ether. Start there. Squint to the slant of the sun, a game with a magnifying glass. Watch the housekeepers shake open gilded cages so canaries, terrified, still singing, burst forth in a fever of wings, red, yellow, green, to occupy the cultivated spaces of parks. Listen now to the garbled words of pre-lingual children and their over-clear mothers urging, *What do you say* ... Describe her posture beneath the oak tree as she sits in bug-eye sunglasses and her Tokyo haircut. See how she leans back on her elbows in the grass. See muddy-leaved maple trees the colour of dried blood. Hear the loose canaries socialize with sparrows. Feel your denim swelter and your skin cringe. Smell your sweat as you lean back, lift an arm over park bench. You've been so eager on all your starts, walking like a pilgrim or a penitent. Name the sweat behind your knees. Claim the earth underfoot. Seek out shade under bandshells and rocks, turtle shells and in the hot shoe kicked off, now circled by the fat looping housefly. Start with the daylight pier and its procession of ghosts. You can watch them if you squint behind your sunglasses.

Above and Beneath

The gulls are really efforting. You can see gravity pushing down on them, and, looking closely, a patch of sweat where wings are anchored to body. Their shadows trace the water and sometimes drop deeper to join the sea farers and mariners and long distance swimmers and suicides. By night, the cairns have stacked themselves silently so morning walkers wake to monuments. A blue whale cowers in the bottom of Lake Ontario with eyeless fish and shipwrecks. He's raised the water level by three quarters of a foot, and has more than once spouted long distance swimmers from his blowhole. When the sky matches the water in its clarity and weariness, the whale is calm. Content to drift without meaning or heft, in a cloudless, slipstream universe.

Madagascar Dream

The lemurs watched our riverboat with their sepia irises. On the banks crocodiles were sunning themselves in their studded suits, smiles wide and still. Their claws carved and dragged into the mud. Along the river bends they were submerged and devil-eyed, their pupils a godless slit, a fissure through which there was only the hungry void of all cold-blooded creatures. I fired corks and bottle caps at their eyes from the deck of the riverboat. And they sank and swam as black and nimble as shadows, so adept it could make me forget their quick, strangely unencumbered shuffle upon land. The riverboat had gotten me near drunk in Madagascar, the steamy weather playing a trick, making you thirsty for bottled beer and red wine warmer than blood. I'd made a slingshot with my bra, and fired corks to peg the godless, bulbous eyes of the crocs. Seeing one cork fire over the water in what must have looked like bird flight, one of them snapped his jaws in a leap, and devoured it. That was the cork from a bottle the chef had been saving to make crocodile stew. It was good for cooking, but very poor for drink.

Stormwater

Fields and forest bright with something like electricity. Hot-mouthed wind is turning things inside out, putting a strain on the trunks of old trees with curious taproots winding toward underground lakes with water they might never find, but that have been given names by the people who believed in them so much that their children have been lost to the dark and jumbled subterranean currents.

Trip Wire

There's a kind of electric charge in the world today as the buds ready themselves for explosion, a trip wire of wind and sunshine and suddenly it's all green light showering sparks from every tree. In spring, we do our best to ignore it.

Rattray Marsh

Butterfly shoulder blades, skin-sunned and salted with sand, wrestling deadheads from the lake like lampreys or alligators. Mothers stoop for stones, greasy bags of chips, the smell of out-there and boat gas on a clean breeze. Grandmother poses on the shore, avoiding the little overturning waves. In the sand, the scrabble and bits of debris from high tide: pulled roots, branches, leaves dry as parchment. Children scoop at holes and lose their dripping fingers of stone mulch and crushed mussel shells. Out past the horizon, a deeper blue, a wilder blue where the wind picks up and tests white sails. Skirts over cellulite and shirts over bad tattoos. Smell the sunscreen. Don't forget the drifting cigar Chinook, the emptying of tiny speakers, their glam rock tunes. Stay in the easy ebb of the lake, that great protective mother, placid, soothing, mollycoddling and serene, eyes everywhere on every child. She'll hoist one from a tumble and push him to the shore the lip the brink the edge the verge the cuff the bank the berm the slope the wet threshold where he'll bury his feet and throw his stones and breathe the scent of her well-muscled breeze.

When the Streetlights Come On

A kind of spaciousness. Dusk when bowers open up and snaking streets straighten their backs. The rabbits hunch and speculate. They formulate plans based on worst case scenarios. Always prudent.

Stasis and Sky

The flashlight still crimsons the curving hand, illuminates blood-waves or haunts the bones of the face. Our children, cozy in a mouldy cabin, are held by pines while middle-aged yahoos shout outside their boathouses for *another brewski.* Mosquitos haven't changed their whine either. Same frequency. Returning here, I expected a place of moss-swathed granite cuts, grown over, Jurassic ferns and ancient deer, hobbling on arthritic hocks, where bumper to bumper boat lines held us up for marina ice-cream, where bass had grown the size of rowboats. I expected trees to be three hundred feet tall, hunched with aching backs. The lake would be lower, exposing shipwrecks and bones of old friends, and the tiny succulent blueberries would have spread on scratchy branches, invasive, bearding whole islands. But the insects are still swattable, and deep water still greens in sunbeams, flickers with small silver-sided fish. Moss has only replaced itself. The loon is still yodelling for a mate. These grandchildren-spores moulder the cabin and seagulls hold ancestral memories of the white bread of the nineteen seventies. Stars are utterly indifferent that we've returned. The sky grows deeper and blacker behind them. My children are still sleeping as the beam skims past their perfect fresh faces.

Commuter Train

Railyard. Sleeping and shunting. Place of thieves. Rooftop pigeons smoke butts together. Laugh and cough into their wings. I rode happy, not quite home to him.

Supermarket Liquor Store

I remember shopping at the all-night supermarket and not buying booze. None at all. The little cups of wine for taste were accordion-pleated and largely untouched. A winter fruit fly dozed circles on the surface of the Cabernet Sauvignon and the shopkeeper emitted a low but audible hum. The bottles, amber, dragongreen, crystalline, were prissy as hell. None of them would look at me, not in the state I was in: the trench coat, the zits, the unwashed armpits. But on the outside, I was wearing a spring dress with tiny violets on it, and my legs were smooth and tan, a diamond in each earlobe. My lipstick came from New York on a private jet, and my shoes blew cocaine in VIP lounges in Milano. Still those ignorant bottles were nose up and rude. The low but audible lady behind the counter smiled and let her eyes go all out of focus looking at the claret shelf. The Chardonnay turned its cheek and the Pinot Noir sucked its tongue in disgust. Only the Zinfandel would even speak, mostly blue words, and it was usually *the fucking cheese* this or *the fucking cheese* that. As I left the supermarket the churning winds of suburbia threw handfuls of rocksalt, blew shopping carts to their ribs, wheels spinning, overturned, while night shoppers scanned the air for leather-winged bats, muscled men or banshees. Across the highway dark horses gleamed, just like me, with wetness and with fear.

Between Buildings

Sublime alleyways, a golden road to nothing, sewers and the heat of the laundromat. A dirty window with dreamcatchers and ceramic unicorns in repose—heart failure on them, you can see their pulse in their chests. A used bookstore, volumes breathing. A crow roosts on the balcony looking in with one sharp yellow eye. He's claimed the folding chair for himself and covets my silk stockings, holding one in his fountain-pen beak. I drape elastic on the sofa and his eye twitches like an electronic camera, outraged by my movements, deep in surveillance. We make a deal with each other not to tell.

Bog

Peaty morass. Hip-waders, bog-sucked. The molasses of it. The creosote logs, the underthings choke and sputter in their swimming. Above, sunlight. You can sense it. But the canopy of evergreen holds it aloft and shoves us back under shadow, hand on the back of the neck. Reach an arm under. Maybe you'll grasp a bone. Bog lady. There are so many of us down there with our spooky looks and sodden books. Maybe you'll pull her up, broken and at angles. Her porcelain jaw drags so dirtily. She empties you like sludge from her ocular holes.

Neurotic Creatures

Seahorse impersonators
A difficult robin
Acorns with paranoia
Suffering shellfish
Beleaguered beluga
Water lilies that tell white lies
A cluster of gossiping stars
An antisocial kitten
Narcoleptic sky
Stuttering waves
A fragile bull, weeping
Angsty pinecones
Nests that hoard
Thieving lichen
Loose moss
A dragonfly wracked with self-doubt
A river that perpetually forgets its line, and repeats itself.

Reading in the Bathtub

—for S.M.

Frangipani, white scent, the blossoms like a part of a woman that is both eternal and internal, the smell of the lobe of a perfumed ear, the jangle of an earring, hair in fragranced wafts and his scarf tied tight in a knot at his neck. The beauty of this boy who dresses in chiffon and silk his mother never gave to him. Teak skin, buttered, soft and hairless. Muscled as a young tomcat, but smooth. I label houses condemned. Put the stake in the ground while the laughing madwoman wields pins and butterfly wings as her weapons against unwilling flight. Graceless in the afternoon, they sweat together, fanning themselves elaborate, and the madwoman's hair trickles against her forehead. He powders her. He pins hair back with his dove hands and she lets him. I sink into the bathtub with them, sweating there under Mala's tree, inches from bursting into jasmine, into stars of white flowers, into dangling frangipani, into love songs for other men. It's hard to leave them with the bones in the cellar and all their unfinished business with each other. Where the cleaver? Where the lover? Where the bed linens to be changed? Where the curry meal? Where the spider silk? Where the scarf he stole from mother? I can huddle them together, but only temporarily. She will always rise like the dead in her winding sheet, to build upon the wall of furniture, pushing bedpans into little cracks. And he will starch his uniform and daub behind his ears a most irresistible perfume that his lover will recognize as cereus.

Pond Clock

As frogs emerge from slippery green crevasses, the water lilies purse their lips as if to whistle, as if to call forth the yellow day, but instead they blow out the candle of the sun.

The Movement of Stars

Stars are not stationary, they have legs and wander in sandals.
Stars are not stationary, they have wobbling heads, they have breath and sighs that shake them.
Stars are not stationary, they surge in time with inner music.
Stars are not stationary, they travel in the ways of slow footed philosophers.
Stars are not stationary, they grind in circular ruts deeper as they go.
Stars are not stationary, they pivot on axis—peripherally.
Stars are not stationary, they find their way into bodies of women and babies.
Stars are not stationary, they have replaced the third eye.
Stars are not stationary, they are forever recalculating.

Acknowledgements

My sincere thanks and deep gratitude to all who have made possible the publication of this book:

To *Rhino* in which "Hummingbird Incarnation" first appeared, and to *The Harpweaver* in which "Trespass" first appeared. Thanks as well to Susie Berg for including "Marooned," "Mansions of Plywood," and "This is About the Forest" in her forthcoming anthology *Catherines the Great*.

To the Ontario Arts Council and to Arc Poetry in particular for a Writers Reserve Grant that helped make possible the writing of this book.

To Lillian Allen: for her inspiration, guidance, love and support. Thanks to Melanie Janisse-Barlow for solidarity, friendship, cricket cages, and help navigating these sometimes-murky literary waters.

Deepest gratitude to my Love, AJ. And always, thanks to my boys, Liam and Gabriel. Thanks as well to my extended family for their support.

To the ladies: Ainsley Burns, Charlotte Osborne, Lisa Pennycook, Jenny Strodl, Katie Kaufman, Jowita Bydlowska, Maggie Jansen, Stephanie Black, OCADU colleagues and 12&12 friends. Special thanks to my Mom, for watching the kids while I write.

To the artists: Justin Black for taking time out from big, badass projects to do his auntie's author shot, and to Marlee Jennings for her spectacular, whimsical cover art.

To Elana Wolff, my dear editor, for your encouragement, precision, passion and expertise.

Finally, my gratitude to Michael Mirolla and Connie McParland and all the folks at Guernica for giving me a literary home, and for believing in this book.

About the Author

CATHERINE BLACK is a graduate of the MFA Writing program at The School of the Art Institute of Chicago. Her prose and poetry have appeared in literary journals including *The Fiddlehead, Scrivener Creative Review, The Harpweaver, Palimpsest Journal* and *Rhino,* and her prose poetry will soon be anthologized in *Catherines the Great.* Her first book, *Lessons of Chaos and Disaster*, was published with Guernica Editions in 2007 as the second book in the First Poets Series; her experimental memoir *A Hard Gold Thread,* was published as the first book in Guernica Edition's First Fictions Series and was nominated for the ReLit award. While poetry remains her first love, Catherine has recently ended an affair with her first novel, had a fling with lyric nonfiction on the theme of motherhood and 'madness,' and now things are getting serious with her second novel. Catherine teaches creative writing in OCAD University's BFA Creative Writing program and lives with her family on the edge of the woods in suburbia.

Printed in May 2019
by Gauvin Press,
Gatineau, Québec